ISBN: 0692233326
ISBN 13: 9780692233320
Library of Congress Control Number: 2014912257
Original Works, Chico, CA

THE JOURNEY OF
Nico the Gray Whale

By David Kraatz

Illustrated by Mauricio Forero

One frigid afternoon in the Chukchi Sea a pod of gray whales basked in the dwindling rays of the Arctic sunlight. Untamed winds whipped furiously around the rocky coves. Random snow storms blanketed the sky in wild snow flurries. Piano-sized icebergs called "growlers" crowded the waterways. The end of summer was quickly approaching, ushering in the bitter cold of the Arctic winter.

The whales sensed the change and stirred with anticipation. It was time to leave the cove. The whales departed on the longest annual migration in the animal kingdom. They would travel about 6,000 miles from the Chukchi Sea to the warm lagoons of Baja California, Mexico where the females would give birth to their young.

$\mathcal{N}$ico, the youngest of the pod, was a rambunctious, energetic calf barely a year old. His skin was a mottled black and gray color; his eyes clear and blue, and his mouth carried a playful grin. Nico was rare to the world of whales-he was born blind. Although he could not see, he used echolocation (eh-ko-low-kay-shun) to survive, high frequency sound waves that reverberated off foreign objects. These sound waves enabled Nico to identify the objects, estimate their size and shape at great distances. All the whales departed that afternoon, all except Nico who was accidentally left behind. At dusk, Nico came to his senses. He called out for his pod but there was no response. Nico swam back and forth in the cove searching, nervously calling out for them. It was no use-they were long gone.

2

Nico swam silently out of the cove. Using his ecolocation he tested the depth. He was now entering deeper, colder water. Soon he sensed a pod of whales. He was trying hard to locate his family, and so he called out......

"Whale, whale

Are you like me?

Do you jump with a thump?

Is your skin black or dark grey?

Do you migrate to warmer seas?"

"We swim fast and we swim deep but we are unique. We have two teeth, one of which develops into a spiral tusk on the front of our head. It can grow to be nine feet long. Male narwhals use the tusk to determine social rank and to compete for mates. We are narwhal whales. We are not like you."

In the Bering Sea, northeast Alaska, chunks of ice floated by. Minutes later, Nico again sensed a large pod of whales. Eagerly, he asked:

"Whale, whale

Are you like me?

Do you jump with a thump?

Is your skin black or dark grey?

Do you migrate to warmer seas?"

This time, Nico heard whistling. "We swim fast and we swim deep but we are unique. Our skin is all white. We are known as the "sea canaries" due to the extraordinary variety of whale calls we use to communicate. We are beluga (baa-LOO-ga) whales. We are not like you."

ear the Gulf of Alaska, the
growlers disappeared and
the water was not quite as
frigid. Nico heard the clicks
of an approaching group of
whales. Happily, he asked:

"Whale, whale
Are you like me?

Do you jump with
a thump?

Is your skin black
or dark grey?

Do you migrate to
warmer seas?"

" **W**e swim fast and we swim deep but we are unique. We are the largest of all whales, growing to over 100 feet in length. We eat up to 4,400 pounds of krill (small shrimp-like creatures) every day. We are blue whales. We are not like you."

Off the coast of Canada, Nico encountered another pod of whales. Energetically, he asked:

"Whale, whale

Are you like me?

Do you jump with a thump?

Is your skin black or dark grey?

Do you migrate to warmer seas?"

"We swim fast and we swim deep but we are unique. Our heads are ⅓ the length of our bodies. We are the rarest of all large whales. We are North Pacific right whales. We are not like you."

Along the coast of Washington, Nico came across a large pod of whales. Joyously, he clicked:

"Whale, whale

Are you like me?

Do you jump with a thump?

Is your skin black or dark grey?

Do you migrate to warmer seas?"

"We swim fast and we swim deep but we are unique. We have been compared to the "cheetahs" of large whales. We can swim at great speeds, 22 mph (35 kph) over short distances, making us faster than dolphins. Also, we use baleen, long flat plates, made of fingernail-like material called keratin that hang down from our upper jaws, to trap krill and plankton to eat. We are sei (sigh) whales. We are not like you."

Off the Oregon coast, Nico heard some loud grunts and groans. He imagined that the sounds must be from a pod of whales, so he excitedly asked:

"Whale, whale

Are you like me?

Do you jump with a thump?

Is your skin black or dark grey?

Do you migrate to warmer seas?"

"We swim fast and we swim deep but we are unique. We have a humped back and enormous front flippers. We also love to sing beautiful songs underwater. Our songs can be heard over 3,000 miles (4,828 kilometers) away. We are humpback whales. We are not like you."

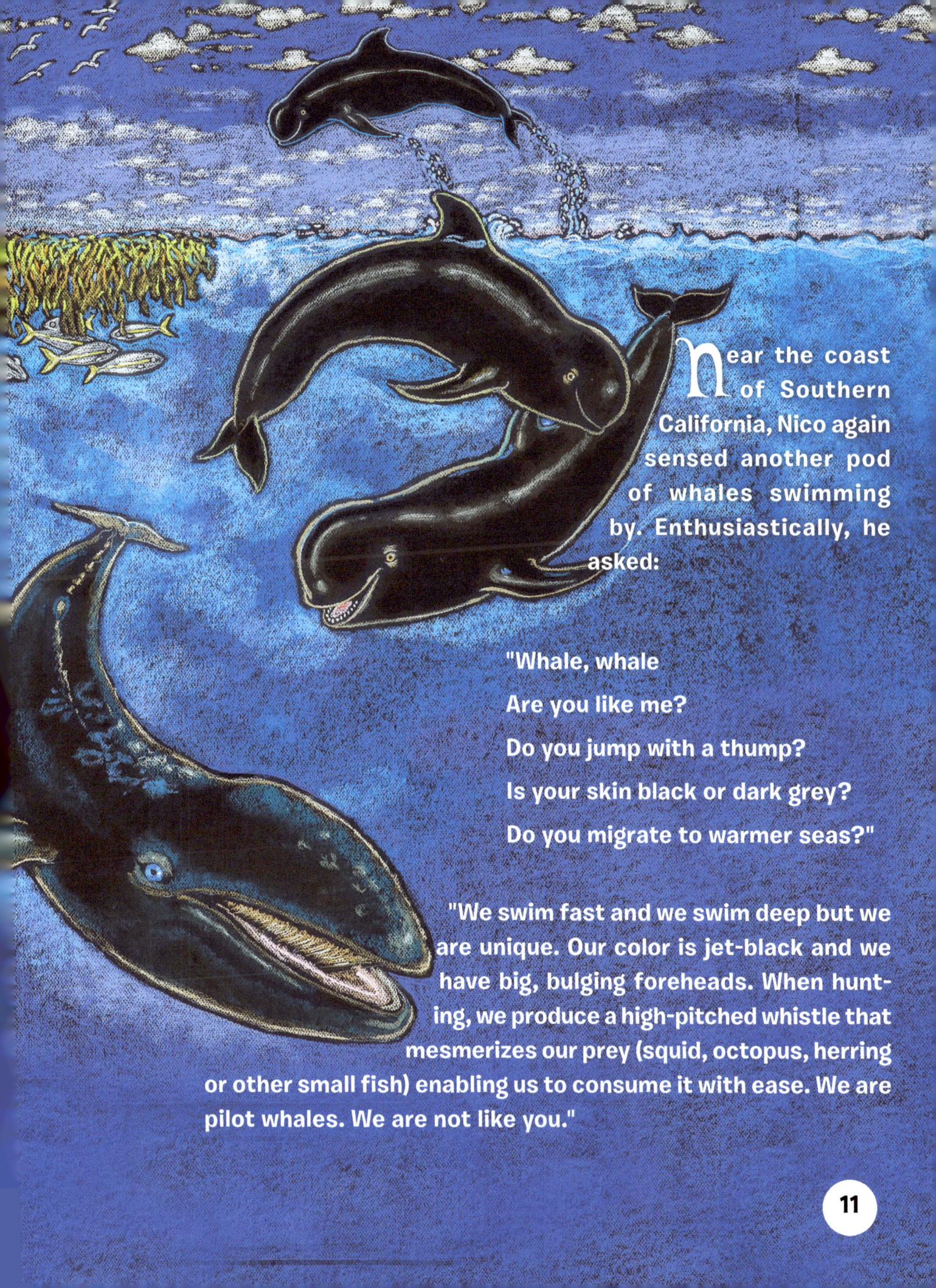

ℕear the coast of Southern California, Nico again sensed another pod of whales swimming by. Enthusiastically, he asked:

"Whale, whale

Are you like me?

Do you jump with a thump?

Is your skin black or dark grey?

Do you migrate to warmer seas?"

"We swim fast and we swim deep but we are unique. Our color is jet-black and we have big, bulging foreheads. When hunting, we produce a high-pitched whistle that mesmerizes our prey (squid, octopus, herring or other small fish) enabling us to consume it with ease. We are pilot whales. We are not like you."

11

Off the coast of Baja California, Mexico, Nico inhaled deeply, descending far below the surface. Suddenly, Nico came upon several large whales. Curiously, he asked:

"Whale, whale

Are you like me?

Do you jump with a thump?

Is your skin black or dark grey?

Do you migrate to warmer seas?"

"We swim fast and we swim deep but we are unique. We are the largest of the toothed whales. We can dive down over one 2,640 feet (804 meters) to feed on squids, octopuses and cuttlefish. We are sperm whales. We are not like you."

nine weeks had passed since Nico had left the Chukchi Sea in search of his family. He had weathered freezing Alaskan storms, escaped marauding sharks, and travelled nearly 6,000 miles. Nico was becoming very frustrated. Where has my family gone? he wondered. The ocean is so immense, he thought. Will I ever find my family again?

earing San Ignacio Lagoon, a large pod of whales passed him in the distance. Instinctively, Nico asked:

"Whale, whale

Are you like me?

Do you jump with a thump?

Is your skin black or dark grey?

Do you migrate to warmer seas?"

"Little whale, little whale

Just like you.....

We swim fast and we swim deep, and we are unique.

We jump with a thump.

Our skin is black or dark gray, and we do migrate to warmer seas.

We are gray whales, voyagers of the open sea. "

15

A large female whale swam forward, "Nico, is that you?" "Yes, it is me, Nico." "I can't believe you survived!" said his mother. "Welcome home, son!" Full of joy, Nico dove to the bottom of the lagoon, sped quickly to the surface and breached, landing with a resounding thump!

GRAY WHALES

When do gray whales make their yearly migration?
In October, gray whales leave their feeding grounds in the Bering and Chukchi Seas. They swim south during the fall and winter to their mating and calving lagoons in Baja California, Mexico. They travel to these warmer waters to give birth. The southward journey takes 2-3 months. The whales return north during the late winter and spring (mid-February to early June).

How fast do gray whales travel during migration?
Gray whales travel at about 2-6 miles per hour (3-10 km/hour) but can reach speeds up to 10-11 miles per hour (16-18 km/hour). They can cover nearly 100 miles (161 km) a day.

How far do gray whales travel?
Gray whales migrate farther than any marine mammal here on earth. Each year they travel 10,000-12,000 miles (16,093-19,312 kilometers) roundtrip between their feeding grounds in the Bering and Chukchi Seas of Alaska to their breeding grounds of Baja California, Mexico.

How large are gray whales?
Adult gray whales reach a maximum length and weight of about 48 feet (14 meters) and 80,000 pounds (36,287 kilograms). Gray whale calves are at most, 16 feet long (5 meters) when they are born and can weigh up to 1,500 pounds (680 kilograms).

How many gray whales are left in the world?
The West Pacific gray whale stock is the most endangered in the world. It hovers on the edge of extinction with just over 100 remaining. The Eastern Pacific gray whale stock is around 21,000 whales and the Atlantic gray whale stock is now extinct. Today, gray whales are protected by international law, and their numbers have grown. In 1994, the gray whale was removed from the United States endangered species list.

What do they eat?
Gray whales are benthic feeders, meaning they feed on the bottom of the ocean. Gray whales dive to the bottom, roll onto their side, and then suck bottom sediments and water into their mouths. Gray whales eat tube worms found in bottom sediments, plankton, mollusks, and small crustaceans by feeding this way.

DEPTH OF KNOWLEDGE QUESTIONS:

1. Recall/Reproduction

* Where were the whales at the beginning of the story?
  (Chukchi Sea)

* Why did the whales leave the Chukchi Sea?
  (Females would give birth to young)

* When did the whales leave the Chukchi Sea?
  (The beginning or the Arctic winter/fall)

* Describe a growler
  (piano-sized iceberg)

* How far did they travel from the Chukchi Sea to the lagoons of Baja California?
  (6,000 miles)

* Which whale can travel the fastest?
  (Sei whale, up to 22 mph)

* How many pounds of krill does a blue whale eat every day?
  (4,400 pounds)

2. Skill/Concept

* Calculate how far the gray whale's round trip would be.
  (12,000 miles)

* If a right whale's head is $1/3$ the length of its body, what is the remaining fraction?
  ($2/3$)

* Compare/contrast narwhal and beluga whales.
  (Answers may vary)

* Describe the challenges a blind whale might encounter while trying to survive on its own. (Answers may vary)

* Explain why gray whales frequently travel in pods.
  (Protection from predators, hunting efficiency, family support)

* Analyze why does the gray whale choose to travel such great distances?
  (To locate better food sources, and find warm, protected waters for calving)

* Justify why sperm whales need to travel $1/2$ mile down to feed.
  (Larger prey-giant squid)

3. Strategic Thinking

* Infer why whales communicate using clicks instead of yelling.
  (Sound travels greater distances under water)

* Explain why the largest creature in the world, the blue whale, would eat
  such a small animal as krill.
  (Krill are more prevalent in cold waters and easier to catch; they are also
  very nutritious)

* Identify the author's purpose for writing this story.
  (To provide information about the migration of the gray whale and
  other whales)

* Which whale would have a better chance of surviving- a baleen (krill-eating)
  or toothed whale? Explain.
  (Answers may vary)

4. Extended Thinking

* What can humans learn about the shape of the whale's body that can
   benefit mankind?
  (Improved aerodynamics)

* In this book, which whale is best adapted to survive and why?
  (Answers may vary)

* If you were a whale, what kind of whale would you be and why? Explain.
  (Answers may vary)

* What is the probability of a single blind gray whale travelling alone from
  the Chukchi Sea to Baja California and surviving?
  (Answers may vary)

* Describe how pollution might affect the survival of the beluga whale.
  (Green house gases cause the temperature to increase, melting the ice,
  affecting food supply)

www.ingramcontent.com/pod-product-compliance
Lightning Source LLC
Chambersburg PA
CBHW060840270326
41933CB00002B/152